Jesus Is Alive

Jesus Is Alive

By Elizabeth Friedrich

Illustrated By Karen Pauls

CPH.
SAINT LOUIS

Copyright © 1987 Concordia Publishing House
3558 S. Jefferson Avenue, St. Louis, MO 63118-3968
Manufactured in the United States of America

Library of Congress Cataloging in Publication Data

Friedrich, Elizabeth, 1949–
    Jesus is alive.

    "Based on materials contained in The story of God's love, c1984"—T.p. verso.
    Summary: Recounts the events surrounding the Resurrection of Jesus Christ.
    1. Jesus Christ—Resurrection—Juvenile literature. [1. Jesus Christ—Resurrection. 2. Bible stories—N.T.] I. Title.
BT481.F734 1987   232.9′7   87-11628
ISBN 0-570-04169-4

5 6 7 8 9 10 11 12 13 14   06 05 04 03 02 01 00 99 98 97

Presented To

Jasheena Kemp

from

Mom & Dad Kemp

Date 4/15/01

Jesus and His disciples were going to Jerusalem. They wanted to be in Jerusalem before the Passover feast on Thursday.

Jesus knew that this would be a special Passover feast because it would be His last Passover. His time on earth was almost over.

After they ate supper, Jesus took His disciples to the Garden of Gethsemane. Jesus told them, "Stay here while I pray."

Jesus walked on alone. He fell to the ground and prayed, "Father, I will do anything You want Me to do." Then God sent an angel to help Jesus feel strong.

When Jesus went back to His disciples, He told them, "Get up. It is time for My enemies to take Me away. Look, here they come now!"

Then the enemies came up to Jesus and arrested Him.

Early the next morning, on Friday, they took Jesus to Pontius Pilate. He was the only ruler who could order people to be put to death.

He told his soldiers to take Jesus and crucify Him.

There on the cross Jesus suffered
to pay for the sins of the world.
After some hours Jesus died.

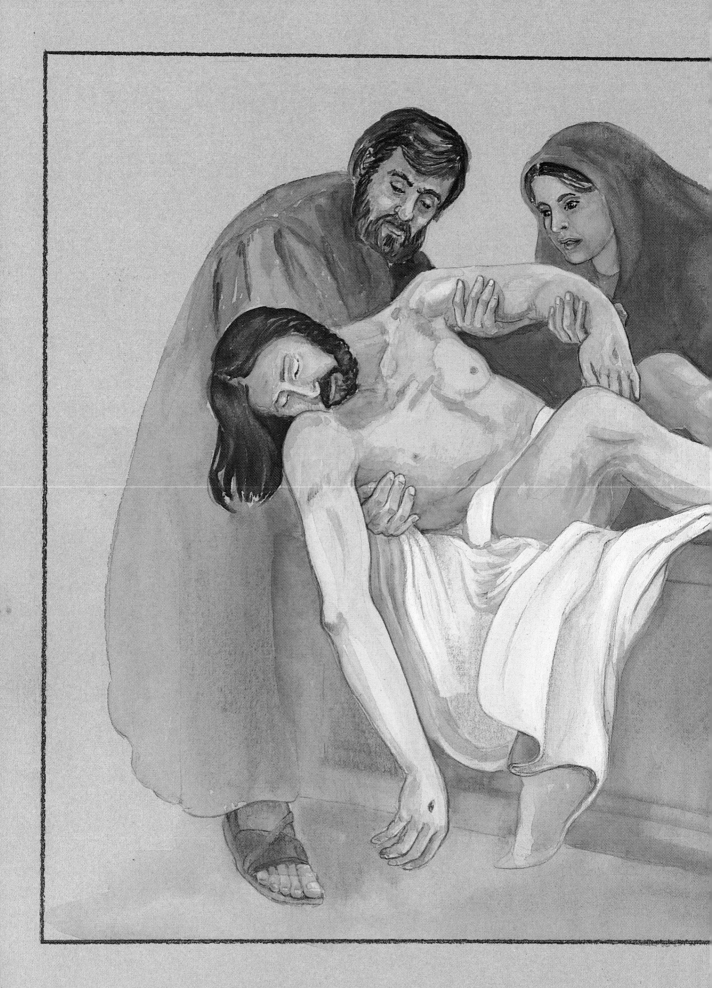

Then some friends of Jesus took His body from the cross. They wrapped it in cloth and laid it in a grave. They closed the door to the grave with a large stone. Pilate sent soldiers to guard the grave of Jesus.

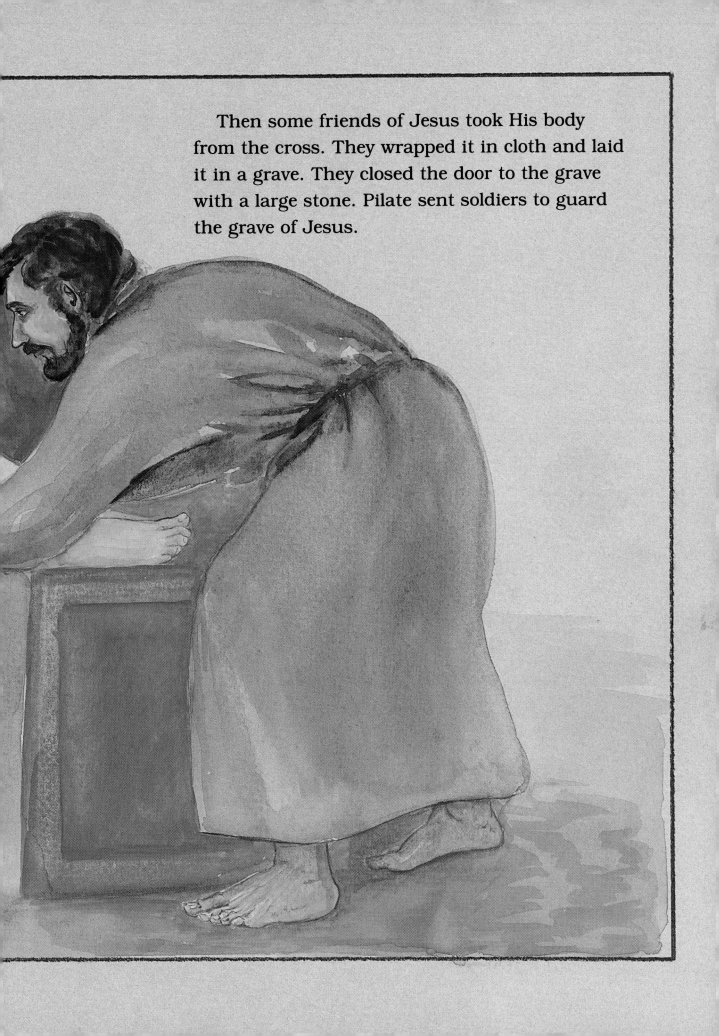

Very early Sunday morning the ground shook.
A bright shining angel came from heaven. He
rolled the stone away from the grave.

The soldiers were very scared. They fell to the
ground. Then they ran away.

Some women were walking to the grave that morning. They carried spices to put on Jesus' body.

They asked one another, "Who will roll the big stone away for us?"

But when the women got there, they saw that the stone had been rolled away. And all the soldiers had left.

Mary Magdalene thought someone had taken Jesus. She went to tell Peter and John.

The other women looked into the grave. They saw two angels.

One angel said, "I know you are looking for Jesus. But He is not here. He has arisen, just as He said He would. Go and tell His disciples."

At once the women ran to tell the disciples.
Mary Magdalene did not know that Jesus had
risen. She told Peter and John that His body was
missing.

Peter and John ran to the grave. Mary followed behind.

They saw the cloth Jesus had been wrapped in. It was folded neatly. But they did not see Jesus. And they did not see the angels.

Then Peter and John went home, but Mary stayed by Jesus' grave.

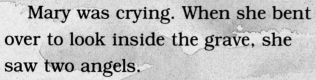

Mary was crying. When she bent over to look inside the grave, she saw two angels.

One of them asked her, "Why are you crying?"

Mary answered, "Jesus is missing. They have taken Him away. I don't know where He is."

Just then Mary turned around. She saw a man standing behind her. Mary thought he was the gardener.

He asked, "Who are you looking for?"

Mary said, "If you took Jesus away, tell me where you have put Him."

The man said, "Mary!"
Now Mary knew He was Jesus.
She cried, "Master! My dear Lord!"
Now Mary was so happy!
Jesus told her, "Tell My
disciples that I am alive."

Later that same day two men walked toward Emmaus. That town was about seven miles from the city of Jerusalem.

Suddenly a man came up and walked with them. It was Jesus, but they did not know Him. He asked, "What are you talking about?"

One of them asked, "Don't You know what happened? Three days ago some soldiers nailed Jesus to a cross, and He died."

Jesus said, "Why don't you believe God's Word? God planned for Jesus to die. That is how He was to save all people from sin. Now Jesus has risen, and He will go to heaven."

At last they came to Emmaus. The two men stopped, but Jesus acted as if He would go on.

The men begged Jesus, "Please stay with us. It is very late."

So Jesus went into the house. The men set out food to eat. Jesus picked up the bread and blessed it. He broke it and gave it to them.

Suddenly the two men knew He was Jesus. Just as quickly Jesus went away. They could not see Him anymore.

Then the two men got up and hurried all the way back to Jerusalem. They knocked on the door where the disciples were meeting.

The two men said, "Jesus really has risen! We walked with Him. We talked with Him. We even had supper with Him. Jesus is alive!"

The disciples were together in that room.
Suddenly Jesus Himself stood in the room
with them.

He said, "Peace be with you."

The disciples were afraid. They thought He was a ghost.

Jesus asked, "Why are you afraid? I am not a ghost. Ghosts don't have skin and bones. Look at My hands and feet. Feel the places where they nailed Me to the cross."

Then Jesus told them, "My Father sent Me to take away the sins of the world. Now I send you.

"Tell all people what you have seen. I will give you the Holy Spirit. He will help you in your work."

Then Jesus went away.

Now the disciples were sure that Jesus was alive. He had risen from the dead.

That Sunday we call Easter. Now every Easter
and every day we praise God because
Jesus Is Alive